DIESELS IN THE WESTERN REGION

GEORGE WOODS

AMBERLEY

First published 2021

Amberley Publishing
The Hill, Stroud
Gloucestershire, GL5 4EP

www.amberley-books.com

Copyright © George Woods, 2021

The right of George Woods to be identified as
the Author of this work has been asserted in
accordance with the Copyrights, Designs and
Patents Act 1988.

ISBN 978 1 3981 0195 1 (print)
ISBN 978 1 3981 0196 8 (ebook)

British Library Cataloguing in Publication Data.
A catalogue record for this book is available from
the British Library.

Origination by Amberley Publishing.
Printed in the UK.

Introduction

The Great Western was always different to the other railways in the UK. When Brunel built the GWR main line from London to Bristol, he laid its track to the broad gauge of 7 feet, when other railways being built in the UK at the same time were using the standard gauge of 4 feet 8.5 inches. Its steam locomotives were not only different in looks, but also differed mechanically in many ways. The Great Western Railway, or God's Wonderful Railway as it was affectionately known, considered itself to be the finest in the land, and up until the early 1930s it probably was, but the other companies were gradually catching up and by the start of the Second World War in 1939, the GWR was starting to fall behind. Even when the railways were nationalised in 1948, the GWR was the only one of the big four to come through virtually unchanged, as they retained much of their former territory and rolling stock so were able to maintain their individuality and carry on their differences well into BR days.

With the advent of the Modernisation Plan of 1956 the Western Region, as it had by then become, kept up the differences by ordering diesel hydraulic locos when the other BR regions all went for diesel electrics, and it was not until the last of the hydraulics were withdrawn in the mid-1970s that the Western finally fell into line with the rest of BR.

Even today, the Great Western atmosphere still survives: the great stations designed by Brunel at Paddington and Temple Meads, which serve his railway from London to Bristol, still exude the feeling of grandeur and quality intended by the designer. One hundred and sixty years after his death, he is still widely celebrated as one of the greatest engineers to have lived.

His talents were many: he was responsible for the design of bridges, steamships, and many civil engineering projects. The Clifton Suspension Bridge along with his giant steamship the *Great Britain* can both still be seen in Bristol, and the Royal Albert rail bridge, opened in 1859, which spans the River Tamar, is still in daily use along with many other bridges and tunnels.

The Great Western first looked at alternatives to steam power before the Second World War, but had to wait until 1946 before it could order a gas turbine loco, No. 18000, of 2,500 hp from the Swiss company Brown Boveri, and another, No. 18100, of 3,000 hp from Metropolitan Vickers in the UK, which was delivered in 1951. The locos were not a great success because their heavy fuel consumption made them uneconomical to operate, plus they were very noisy and none too reliable in everyday service. They were withdrawn from service in 1958 and 1960.

Apart from two diesel shunters the only diesels run by the GWR was a fleet of thirty-eight diesel railcars introduced in the 1930s. These proved very successful and were used in branch line service and for shorter cross-country journeys, remaining in service into the early 1960s.

The first diesel locomotives to be introduced were five North British-built A1A-A1A 2,000 hp locos and fifty-two Bo-Bo 1,000 hp locos, all using MAN diesel engines with hydraulic transmissions, which started to enter service in 1958. These two types proved unreliable in service and were withdrawn in the early 1970s. The 2,000 hp locos were built on a heavy chassis, but the Western Region management came to an agreement with MAN, the German manufacturers, to develop a UK version of the V200 Bo-Bo locos then in service in Germany. Thirty-eight of this type, which became BR Class 42, were ordered using Maybach engines and were constructed with a lightweight prestressed body, which weighed 30 tons less than the original five locos, and were built by British Railways at Swindon, entering service from 1958. A further thirty-three similar locos were built by North British in Glasgow between 1960 and 1962 and became BR Class 43.

The need for a mixed-traffic loco was met by the introduction of the Hymek 1,750 hp Bo-Bo type, powered by a Maybach 1,750 hp engine with Mekydro hydraulic transmission. A total of 101 were built by Beyer Peacock between 1961 and 1964, and they became the most successful of the hydraulic designs. They were among the first BR diesels to benefit from an outside industrial design consultant and were a distinct improvement in looks and styling over the previous diesel types.

Along with the Eastern Region of BR, it was realised that 2,000 hp was not enough power to operate the faster trains that the public were demanding, so the 2,700 hp Western Co-Co Class 52 was developed. The Westerns were powered by two 1,350 hp Maybach engines with Voith hydraulic transmissions, and seventy-four were built at Crewe and Swindon works, entering service between 1961 and 1964. These too benefitted from the design consultants and were regarded as the best-looking BR diesel design introduced up until then. They became a firm favourite with enthusiasts because of their good looks, and also the distinctive noise they made when working hard. They were more reliable in service but suffered some problems with engines and transmissions.

In 1968 the BR policy was changed to standardise the use of diesel electric locos, which made the use of hydraulic locos on the Western more expensive, as there were many extra costs in maintaining non-standard types. Another reason for early withdrawal was the introduction of air-conditioned coaches on InterCity services, which required an electricity supply from the locomotive, easily achieved with diesel electrics but would have entailed expensive modifications to the hydraulic locos. When the 2,750 hp Brush type 4 (Class 47) diesel electrics were introduced from 1963, these were gradually introduced on to the Western and replaced the hydraulic types, along with the introduction of Class 50s, which were made redundant by the WCML Electrification in 1974, and the InterCity 125s in 1977 spelt the end for the Class 52s and the hydraulic experiment.

Opinion is mixed on the relative merits of hydraulic vs electric transmissions: some say that the lighter weight and easier maintenance of hydraulic locos outweighs the complication of the diesel electric types, but these could produce higher horsepower and were capable of being worked for long periods at or near full power without the overheating issues experienced by the hydraulics.

BR was following American experience where the electric transmission has ruled the roost since the introduction of the first diesel locos in 1925, apart from experiments with some German hydraulic locos by the Southern Pacific in the 1960s, which showed many of the same problems experienced in the UK.

The British Railways Modernisation Plan of 1955 aimed to do away with steam traction in the mid-1970s, but the Western Region became the first part of BR to completely do away with its steam fleet, which it accomplished in early 1966. From 1956 it had introduced diesel multiple units (DMUs) on many of its cross-country services such as Birmingham to Cardiff and Penzance to Plymouth and Exeter. The first part of the Western to become completely diesel worked were the far west lines in Devon and Cornwall, which saw their last steam workings in 1964.

Dieselisation of the suburban services from Paddington to Reading began in 1958 and was largely completed in 1961. Another large part of the Western to see the introduction of DMUs at about the same time were the local services in the South Wales Valleys centred on Newport and Cardiff.

From 1958 the diesels gradually took over the haulage of the important express services and in 1963 the last steam-hauled route from Paddington to Worcester succumbed to the diesel invasion. The very last steam-hauled passenger train, the 16.38 Paddington to Banbury, hauled by 7029 *Clun Castle*, ran on 11 June 1965, but some steam-hauled freights lasted until the end of Western steam in 1966.

What was probably the most important event in recent Western history was the introduction of the InterCity 125, which started service on the routes to Bristol and South Wales in 1976, with the West Country trains to Plymouth and Penzance following soon after. These trains were a great success, running until the electrics took over forty-three years later in 2019.

In 1993 it was announced that a fast electric train service would connect Paddington with Heathrow Airport, and the first services started in 1998. Then in 2012 (things happen fast in the UK) it was announced that the Great Western lines from Paddington to Bristol and South Wales would be electrified, and the first services began in 2018 using Hitachi-designed trains, which were bi-powered (i.e. not only by electric motors but by diesel engines so as to be able to work on non-electrified routes). So twenty years after the Heathrow services commenced the main line services from Paddington were finally brought up to modern standards. Brunel would have been pleased, but I bet he would have achieved these results a lot quicker.

Abbreviations
BR: British Railways
BSC: British Steel Corporation
ECS: Empty Carriage Stock
ELR: East Lancashire Railway
LCGB: Locomotive Club of Great Britain
LNWR: London North Western Railway
MAN: Maschinenfabrik Augsburg Nurnberg
MPD: Motive Power Depot
NBL: North British Locomotive Company Glasgow
NCB: National Coal Board
NYMR: North Yorkshire Moors Railway
WCML: West Coast Main Line

Great Western railcar No. 22 was built in 1940 and withdrawn from service in 1962, and is seen at the Didcot Railway Centre on 24 August 2017. It was one of thirty-eight railcars built by the GWR between 1934 and 1962 for service on branch lines and shorter secondary services and proved a great success, lasting until replaced by the introduction of the British Railways diesel trains in the early 1960s.

In this typical Western Region scene diesel hydraulic Warship Class D809 *Champion* passes through the city of Bath with a train of coal empties heading for one of the Mendip collieries in May 1969, as a variety of vintage vehicles negotiate a junction on the A36. D809 survived for over two more years, being withdrawn in October 1971 and cut up at Swindon a year later.

18000 at Didcot GWR Railway Centre on 24 August 2017. Nicknamed Kerosene Castle, 18000 was a prototype 2,500 hp gas turbine that was built in Switzerland by Brown Boveri and delivered to BR Western Region in 1949. It had a lot of problems in service but somehow eventually finished up in Vienna from where it was rescued and returned to the UK in the early 1990s.

Seen here at Barry MPD on 8 September 1968, D9528 was one of fifty-six Class 14 diesel hydraulic locos built at Swindon in 1964–65. They were intended for trip freights and heavy shunting duties, but by the time the order was completed this type of work was fast disappearing from BR and most of them finished up in industrial service.

D9502 also finished up with the NCB, in Northumberland, and is here seen crossing the level crossing near the Burradon Social Club on 9 May 1969. It has since been preserved at the East Lancashire Railway.

D9529 (BSC 61) arrives at Goathland on the NYMR in May 1980. This loco worked at several installations including British Steel at Corby, but is now preserved at the Nene Valley Railway.

D9516 at the Didcot Railway Centre on 24 August 2017. After the end of its BR service in 1968, it worked at BSC Corby before it was preserved in 1981.

D9551 is seen at Bridgnorth on the SVR with the breakdown crane on 9 June 2019. This was another loco that worked at BSC Corby.

D7076 and D9521 are seen at Bury ELR in July 1989. D7076 was built at Beyer Peacock in Manchester in 1963 and withdrawn by BR in 1973. It found use at the Derby Research centre before being preserved. D9521 worked at NCB Ashington after withdrawal by BR and is now preserved at the Dean Forest Railway.

D7045 arrives at Salisbury Station on 14 August 1966 with a parcels train from the Western Region. One hundred and one Hymek Class 35 diesel hydraulic locos were built by Beyer Peacock from 1963. They were the most successful of the hydraulic locos and worked all types of traffic. This loco was scrapped at Swindon in August 1973.

D7082 descends Sway bank on the approach to Brockenhurst with an inter-regional express for Birmingham. Because BR had decided to concentrate on diesel electric locos, the Hymeks had a short life, and after less than ten years of service, this loco was scrapped at Swindon in October 1972.

An immaculate D7004, which has just been overhauled at Swindon and painted in the standard Rail Blue livery of the period, stands at Yeovil Pen Mill Station with an afternoon Weymouth to Bristol train on 7 June 1967. This loco worked for only eleven years before being scrapped at Swindon in August 1972.

The low evening sun catches D7036 as it arrives at Reading with an evening train from Oxford to Paddington on 15 April 1968.

A rather worse for wear D7089 stands at Barry MPD, which had closed in September 1964 but survived as a stabling point for some years after. Taken on 8 September 1968.

D7044 passes a selection of typically Great Western lower quadrant signals as it arrives at Swansea High Street Station with a parcels train in September 1969.

D7026 has just arrived at a very run-down-looking Paddington Station with a train probably from Worcester in March 1972.

D7054 departs from Hereford on 14 October 1972 with a train towards Gloucester and Paddington. The large number of enthusiasts on the bridge are waiting the departure of 5596 *Bahamas* with a steam special.

D7028 and D7001 are seen at Worcester Shrub Hill Station with the Hymek Swansong Railtour from Paddington to Bristol, Abergavenny, Evesham and back to Paddington on 22 September 1973.

Class 42 D821 *Greyhound* passes through Woking cutting with a morning express from Exeter Central bound for Waterloo on 14 February 1967.

D868 *Zephyr,* still in its original green livery, passes Worting Junction as it heads for Waterloo with an express from Exeter Central in August 1966. One of the later Class 43s, it was built at Swindon in 1961 and scrapped in 1972.

Class 42 D832 *Onslaught* in later maroon livery heads in the opposite direction at Worting with an express for Exeter on the same day in 1966. D832 was built at Swindon in 1961, has been preserved and can currently be seen at the ELR.

The firemen on D868 *Zephyr* and 34102 *Lapford* watch for their signals to clear as they wait outside Waterloo to back down on to their evening trains in the last week of Southern steam on 4 July 1967. Taken from the flats overlooking the station.

D866 *Zebra* heads west through Brookwood Station with a Waterloo to Exeter train on a dull 14 February 1967. A Class 33 comes into view with a freight in the background.

D847 *Strongbow* waits to back down on to the LCGB Woodpecker Railtour at Reading Station as an identified Western arrives with a Bristol to Paddington train on 20 April 1969.

Three more pictures of D847 *STRONGBOW* on the Woodpecker tour, this time as tour participants sample the delights of the once busy junction at Ashchurch Station. The tour started from Waterloo, and its destination was Bulmers sidings at Hereford where ex-GWR 6000 *King George V* was based at this time.

Taken on a cold 2 December 1967, D811 *Daring* leaves Teignmouth Station with a train heading towards Exeter. We made the winter journey to Devon to follow 6998 and 1450 on their way from Plymouth to the Didcot Railway Centre.

D832 *Onslaught* outside the Railway Technical Centre at Derby where it was employed on research projects. It went from here into preservation on the ELR. Taken on 28 August 1975.

Class 42 D832 at the Crewe Works Open Day on 31 May 2003. The loco was one of thirty-three built by NBL in Glasgow from 1958 to 1961.

Class 42 D821 *Greyhound* and D9529 at Grosmont MPD on the NYMR in October 1982. D821 was preserved after withdrawal from BR in 1972, and was first at Didcot, then the NYMR, and is now based on the SVR.

D821 climbs past Greengates on the NYMR on a sultry day in July 1983 with a train for Pickering.

D821 rolls downhill at Greengates, heading for Grosmont, on its first day back in service on the NYMR after a repaint. The undergrowth is badly burned, probably set alight by sparks from a steam loco climbing the gradient. Taken in May 1984.

D832 and D7076 raise the echoes as they roar up the 1 in 36 gradient towards Goathland Station with a well-loaded train for Pickering during the NYMR Diesel Gala weekend on 6 November 1999.

D1045 *Western Viscount* waits to depart from Paddington in October 1967 with a train for Plymouth. It was built at Swindon in 1962 and scrapped there in 1975.

D1067 *Western Druid* waits to leave Paddington with a Bristol service in May 1969.

An unidentified Western backs its empty train out of Paddington in October 1967. Major track and signalling alterations were being undertaken, hence the piles of ballast on the platform.

D1050 *Western Ruler* is also backing its train out of Paddington in May 1969. Paddington was fortunate to have had carriage sidings close enough for the incoming loco to be able to do this. It also had the loco servicing facilities at Ranelagh Bridge very close by.

D1068 *Western Reliance* looks very smart in its fresh coat of BR blue while leaving Paddington in May 1969. In the background is the huge Paddington Goods Depot, which was demolished in 1986.

D1053 *Western Patriarch* passes Royal Oak Station in May 1969 with a Bristol-bound express. This station is just an island platform served by London Transport Metropolitan Line trains.

The next three pictures were taken in May 1969 at Royal Oak Station. The platform here gave a good view of the activities at the Ranelagh Bridge loco yard, which acted as a servicing point for locos on a quick turnaround in between arrival and departure from neighbouring Paddington. The flats in the background are undergoing a much-needed refurbishment, removing years of grime deposited by the steam locos, which used the facilities here for many years. The yard continued in use until 1980.

D1053 *Western Patriarch* adds to the pollution.

Water overflows from the tank of D1058 *Western Nobleman.*

D1056 *Western Sultan,* D1015 *Western Champion* and D1587 receive attention.

D1067 *Western Druid* departs from Bath Spa Station in May 1969 with a Paddington to Bristol train. The spire of Bath First Spiritualist Church dominates the left of the image.

With the River Avon in the foreground and St Catherine's Church behind, an unidentified Western departs from Bath with a Paddington to Bristol train in May 1969.

Right: The headboard is fixed to a very travel-worn Western as it waits to leave Paddington with the Bristol Venturer Railtour on 12 October 1969.

Below: Part of the itinerary in Bristol was a visit to Bristol Bath Road MPD and the next five pictures show locos undergoing various maintenance procedures. First we have a Western and a Hymek being refuelled.

Above and below: Two pictures showing a Blue Pullman D1067 *Western Druid* and D0280 *Falcon* inside the main maintenance shed. There had been an engine shed on this site since the days of the Bristol and Exeter Railway and the sheds went through many alterations over the years. The diesel depot finally closed in 1995 and the site was earmarked for a major development, which has yet to take place.

Right and below: D8xx, D10xx and D1027 *Western Lancer* stand outside the shed and are ready for their next duties. The depot was ideally placed next to Bristol Temple Meads Station and a good view of the comings and goings could be had from the adjacent platform.

Above and below: D1033 *Western Trooper* arrives and departs from Newton Abbot Station with a Plymouth to Paddington express on 15 October 1975. The introduction of the Westerns sped up services to Plymouth, and in 1964 the Golden Hind express journey time was reduced to three hours and fifty minutes.

Above and below: D1063 *Western Monitor* waits for departure time at a very wet Penzance with a train for Paddington on 16 October 1975. Opened in 1842, Penzance is the terminus of the West of England main line, 327 miles from London Paddington.

The rain at St Erth was even worse and D1063 *Western Monitor* heads into the monsoon with its Paddington-bound train. St Erth is the junction for the branch line to the famous seaside resort of St Ives.

D1063 *Western Monitor* is seen again on 18 October 1975 arriving at Liskeard with the Cornish Riviera Express for Paddington. Liskeard is the junction for the branch line to Looe.

Above and below: These two pictures, taken at Liskeard Station in Cornwall on 16 October 1975, of D1010 *Western Campaigner* working an eastbound parcels train show that the Great Western atmosphere was still to be found as late as 1975. The loco is a pure Western Region design, and the leading vehicle is a GWR siphon parcels van. The signals are typical GWR lower quadrants and the rails are the old bullhead type. The only major change is the BR blue livery, which was applied from 1967, but it wouldn't last for much longer as the Westerns will be gone by 1977, replaced by Class 50s and the InterCity 125. *Western Campaigner* was one of seven Westerns that survived into preservation and can be seen at the West Somerset Railway.

Left: On its way to Plymouth on 18 October 1975, D1063 is seen crossing Isambard Kingdom Brunel's famous Royal Albert Bridge across the River Tamar at Saltash. The bridge was opened in 1859 and carries the West of England main line into Cornwall.

Below: At Plymouth North Road Station D1036 *Western Emperor* has taken over and is departing for Paddington. Plymouth is a major station on the line to Penzance and a station has stood on this site since 1877.

An unidentified Western heads a mixed freight through Southall Station, probably heading for Acton yard, on 27 April 1973. The picture was taken from the footbridge that led to Southall MPD.

D1005 *Western Venturer* passes Reading Station with a westbound freight in May 1976. Coupled to the loco is a brake tender, which was used to provide additional braking power on unfitted freight trains.

D1023 *Western Fusilier* arrives at Reading Station with an additional train for the West Country in May 1976. At this time the train number reporting panels were no longer used for their original purpose and were often used to show the loco number.

D1023 *Western Fusilier* is seen in enemy territory as it waits to leave King's Cross Station on 20 November 1976 with the Western Talisman Railtour bound for York.

Above and below: D1062 *Western Courier*, by now a preserved loco, is seen here at the small engine shed on the South Devon Railway at Paignton on 14 July 1977. Later on the same day D1062 passes along the clifftops near Goodrington Sands with a train for Dartmouth.

D1062 is seen here on 25 August 1980 taking part in the Rainhill Cavalcade, which was organised to celebrate 150 years of Britain's railways.

D1023 *Western Fusilier* has been preserved as part of the National Collection by the NRM at York. The loco is seen at the Crewe Works Open Day, held on 10 September 2005 to celebrate 150 years of building locomotives at the famous workshops.

D1015 *Western Champion* is passing Greenholme on 3 May 2008 and has just started the climb to Shap Summit, 912 feet above sea level. The train is the Western Scot Railtour and the destination is Edinburgh. The loco has been preserved and is in the care of the Diesel Traction Group.

To celebrate its centenary, Eastleigh Works held an open day on 25 May 2009, and among the exhibits was D1015 *Western Champion*.

Above and below: On one of its rare outings from the NRM, D1023 *Western Fusilier* arrives at Oxenhope on the KWVR with a trainload of enthusiasts, and later in the day prepares to depart from Keighley on 7 June 2008.

Above and below: The Western Fellsman Railtour was run on 31 July 2010 from Westbury to Carlisle and return, and was unusual in that D1015 *Western Champion* was renamed on one side as D1038 *Western Sovereign* for one day only. The first picture was taken of the northbound train at Little Salkeld on the WCML, and it returned via the Settle and Carlisle and is seen near Kirkby Thore. Unfortunately D1015 suffered a major failure to one of its engines on the return journey, and was out of traffic for some time for repairs.

The Yuletide East Yorkshireman Railtour was run on 17 December 2016 from Swindon to Scarborough via Hull, and again the loco D1015 *Western Champion* was renamed on one side, this time to D1031 *Western Rifleman*. The train is seen running through the flat East Yorkshire countryside approaching Hutton Cranswick, which lies between Beverley and Driffield.

Above and below: D0280 *Falcon* seen at Reading on 15 April 1968. Built by Brush Traction in 1961, *Falcon* was a one-off prototype 2,880 hp diesel electric loco that used two of the same Maybach diesel engines that powered the Western-type diesel hydraulics, but driving a generator and traction motors. The loco was quite successful, but BR decided on the Sulzer single-engine Class 47 to be its standard type four loco.

Only the motive power has changed as D3604 plus its ex-GWR shunters truck shunts coal wagons at Radyr Station among the GWR signals on 22 July 1969. Western Region steam had finished in South Wales some four years previously, but steam was still in use by the NCB at a few collieries in the area until the mid-1970s.

St Peter's Church dominates the background in this view of D3601 shunting parcels vehicles at Gloucester Station on 20 April 1974. This is the former GWR Central Station, which became the only station in Gloucester after the closure of the former Midland Eastgate Station in 1975.

24076 waits in the loop at Machynlleth Station with a short freight heading towards Pwllheli in July 1977. The third and fourth wagons are gunpowder vans bound for Porthmadog where the contents will be used in the nearby quarries.

25224 departs from Paignton Station with a local service towards Exeter on 15 October 1975. Some Class 25s were transferred to the Western Region in 1971 to replace the diesel hydraulics, which were starting to be withdrawn, and remained in service until the early 1980s.

Above and below: Two views of 25225 at Par Station with a train of china clay wagons, which have been loaded at the nearby English China Clay works. The first shows the train arriving from the works, and the second as it waits to depart westwards. Taken on 17 October 1975.

25169 calls at Liskeard Station with a parcels train bound for Penzance on 18 October 1975. 25169 stayed on the Western for less than a year, as it was transferred to Wigan in August 1976.

25253 and 25261 await departure time at Aberystwyth with the 10.00 Saturday-only through train to London Euston, which they will take as far as Shrewsbury. Taken in August 1977.

5530 passes Royal Oak Station with empty stock from Paddington to the sidings at Old Oak Common in March 1972. The first Class 31s were allocated to the Western Region in 1969 to replace diesel hydraulics.

5826 arrives at Didcot Station with a parcels train heading towards Oxford in March 1972. This loco had been allocated to Bristol Bath Road depot a few months previously, and remained on the Western until it was withdrawn in 1990.

Above and below: Two unidentified Class 31s speed through Reading Station in August 1976. The first was a stock train bound for Old Oak Common sidings in August 1976. The second heads an EnParts train for the MPD at Old Oak Common.

31147 departs from Newton Abbot Station with a westbound parcels train on 15 October 1975. The three Gresley carriages on the right of the picture are alongside the David and Charles Co. Ltd works, who publish a wide range of titles including many on railways.

33008 arrives at Exeter St David's Station with a train from the Plymouth direction on 13 July 1977. 33008 has been preserved and can be seen on the Battlefield line in Leicestershire.

Above and below: 33110 has just taken over a cross-country service from Newcastle to Bournemouth at Reading from 45145, which can be seen to the right. 33110 was one of nineteen locos equipped for push and pull operations. This loco has also been preserved and is currently at the Bodmin and Wenford Railway in Cornwall. Taken in August 1976.

Left: D6876 waits to depart from Radyr with a coal train bound for one of the docks in the Cardiff area on 22 July 1969. Class 37s were introduced to the South Wales Valleys in the early 1960s, replacing the steam locos that were used on the many coal trains from the mines to the docks at Cardiff and various power stations in the area.

Below: D6941 passes the site of Marshfield (Mon.) Station, which lies on the South Wales main line, with a coal train heading towards Cardiff.

Class 37s were rarely seen at Paddington, but sometime in March 1979, 37167 found its way there and waits to depart with a parcels train.

45006 *Honourable Artillery Company* arrives at Newton Abbot with a cross-country service from the north on 15 October 1975. 214 miles from Paddington, Newton Abbot is the junction station for the branch line to the popular Devon resorts of Torquay and Paignton.

Above and below: 46044 runs along the sea wall near Teignmouth with a northbound cross-country service, and soon after 46039 heads towards the west with another cross-country train. Passengers heading to the Devon resorts from the northern cities were always pleased to get to this most scenic part of their journey, as it meant their destination was getting close. Both taken on 15 July 1977.

In a scene that is still full of Great Western atmosphere, 46026 *Leicestershire and Derbyshire Yeomanry* is seen arriving over the Red Cow level crossing at the London end of Exeter St David's Station on 13 July 1977 with an express from the north. On the left is Exeter Middle Box, while the goods transfer shed behind, which dates from 1864, still seems to be in use, and GWR semaphore signals still stand proud.

46026 at Exeter St David's Station awaiting departure with its westbound train on 13 July 1977. The first station here was built in 1844 to serve Brunel's broad gauge Bristol and Exeter Railway, and has undergone many transformations since, the most recent being in 1985, but still retains many earlier features.

46020 arrives at Liskeard Station on 18 October 1975 with a northbound train. The station here is the junction for the branch line to Looe, which somehow avoided being closed by Dr Beeching in the 1960s.

A May 1969 scene at Paddington showing 1659 waiting to depart for Bristol, and a Western prepares to leave with another westbound express. Paddington Station, designed by Brunel, was opened in 1854 with four platforms, but has expanded over the years to fourteen platforms.

A Ford Zephyr, beloved by both villains and police in 1960s movies, heads along the A36 road as 1932 arrives at Bath with a Bristol to Paddington train in May 1969. 1932 is in an early BR blue livery, with BR emblems and numbers at each end of the loco.

Above left and left: 47091 makes a smoky departure from Liskeard with a westbound train, and a few minutes later 47074 arrives with train for Paddington. Both were taken on 18 October 1975.

A Class 47 passes through Par Station with a train from Paddington to Penzance on 17 October 1975. Par is the junction for Newquay, which was another branch line that was lucky to survive the Beeching cuts.

Fresh from overhaul, 47237 waits at Paddington Station to run out to Ranelagh Bridge yard for servicing before its next journey west in August 1976. The large iron bridge carries Bishops Bridge Road over the tracks and was designed by Brunel. The bridge was renewed in 2006.

47113 leaves Reading for Paddington with a failed Class 50 in tow in August 1976. The Class 50s were in a run-down condition when they were transferred to the Western Region and failures were frequent until they were refurbished at Doncaster Works.

47076 *City of Truro* leaves Oxford with a train for Paddington on 29 May 1977. 47076 was one of several Class 47s that were named after famous GWR steam locos.

Fresh from an overhaul at Crewe Works, 47455 passes Shrewsbury Station with a freight heading towards the Wolverhampton line in July 1977. Shrewsbury jail can be seen behind the handsome ex-LNWR signal.

50028 arrives at Reading with a train for Paddington in August 1976. As the Class 50s were refurbished, they followed in the tradition of the Class 42/43 by being named after warships that were based in Plymouth.

A Class 50 stands in the imposing Exeter St David's Station with a westbound express for Paignton on 13 July 1977. St David's is the junction for the lines to Barnstaple and London Waterloo via Salisbury.

50037 departs from Newton Abbott with a westbound service. In the background the MPD is still in use, as are the carriage sidings behind. The scene today is unrecognisable as only three tracks have survived to run through the station. The stone building to the right of the picture is a survivor from the days of the South Devon Railway.

Another Class 50 arrives with a train for Paddington. The view in this direction has not changed so much as separate tracks for the main line to Plymouth and the line to Paignton, which goes off at nearby Aller Junction, still exist. Both pictures were taken on 13 July 1977.

Above and below: Two Class 50s seen passing along the sea wall near Teignmouth on 15 July 1977. The first train is a Paddington express consisting of mark 2F air-conditioned stock, and travelling in the opposite direction is a westbound train headed by 50036, which has just emerged from Parsons Tunnel.

Left: A Class 50 braves the waves as it comes off the sea wall and arrives at Dawlish Station with a train for the west on 15 July 1977. The railway along the sea wall here has always been subject to damage by rough seas, but in 2014 an exceptional storm destroyed a long stretch of railway, closing the line for several months while major repairs were carried out.

Below: Another Class 50 passes along the sea wall near Teignmouth heading an express towards Exeter on 15 July 1977. Plans are also in hand for major works to protect this section of railway from damage by the sea.

Above and right: 56049 is seen passing
two sets of GWR signals as it departs from
Westbury with an associated road stone train
from one of the Mendip Quarries, bound for
Acton Yard in West London in June 1983.
From Acton the stone is distributed to many
destinations in the London area.

57601 in Porterbrook livery is at Paddington Station and has arrived with the carriages to form the 14.30 First Great Western service to Penzance on 17 April 2002.

57604 *Pendennis Castle* at the NRM York Railfest show on 6 June 2012. This loco was repainted into GWR colours to celebrate 175 years of the GWR.

59002 *Alan J Day* passes through Reading Station with a Mendip Rail train of empty aggregate wagons from Acton Yard to Merehead Quarry on 3 June 2004.

59004 *Paul A Hammond* heads a 3,000-ton jumbo yeoman aggregate train from Merehead bound for Acton Yard, passing Twyford on 3 June 2004.

Above and below: Two pictures of Class 59 locos used to haul the aggregate trains from the Somerset quarries, taken at the Eastleigh Works open day on 25 May 2009. The first photo shows 59001 *Yeoman Endeavour* in Aggregate Industries livery, and the second photo shows 59206 *John F Yeoman* in DB Schenker colours.

A Western Pullman stands in Paddington Station awaiting departure time in May 1969. The DMU is not part of the train, just sharing the platform.

Another Western Pullman leaves Paddington on an afternoon service during the period when the original blue livery was being replaced by the blue and grey BR Corporate colours. Taken in May 1969.

Above and below: Two pictures taken in the same position at Cardiff Station but nearly fifty years apart. The first is of the South Wales Pullman, taken on 22 July 1969 during its stop where it is changing drivers on its way from Paddington to Swansea. The second, taken on 23 July 2018, shows 800 016, one of the latest trains in GWR service that is able to run on diesel power, or when under the wires on electric power. It has just arrived from Paddington and after a quick turnround will head back to London.

Above and below: Two more pictures of the South Wales Pullman in its last weeks of service. The first shows the Swansea-bound train passing the site of Marshfield Station on 4 April 1973, and just a week before its withdrawal from service, the Paddington-bound South Wales train speeds through Southall Station on the last leg of its journey on 27 April 1973.

Only a few months after their introduction into service, an InterCity 125 service for Bristol, formed of unit 253 007, waits to depart from Paddington in August 1976.

31118 waits its next duty at Bristol Temple Meads Station and is flanked by InterCity 125 sets 253 001 and 046 in June 1983.

43128, which is still in the original First Great Western livery, known as the fag packet livery, stands at Paddington alongside 332 002 on which is one of the trains operated by Heathrow Express and at that time (17 April 2002) was the only electric service running from Paddington.

A 125 in the second First Great Western livery, with 43022 leading, arrives at Reading on 17 April 2002 with a westbound service.

A picture that shows the fag packet livery in all its glory, as worn by 43164 during its stop at Reading on 3 June 2004. 43164 must have been one of the last power cars to retain these colours, as most of the Great Western 125 fleet had been repainted into the new colours, as seen on the coaches.

By 24 August 2017 yet another First Great Western colour scheme had come into being, which can be seen on 43017, standing at Paddington alongside the fine bronze statue of the father of the Great Western, Isambard Kingdom Brunel. The statue by John Doubleday was unveiled on the station in 1982, but was moved to a more prominent position in 2014.

On 31 May 2019 43192 is seen outside Doncaster Works fresh from refurbishment and wearing what should prove to be the last GWR colour scheme of plain dark green with silver lettering. By this time the GWR 125s were coming to the end of service after the introduction of the 800 series of trains, but some were being used in five-car formations in Cornwall, so hopefully will be with us for some time to come.

A Class 122 single car with a trailer crosses the River Thames shortly after leaving Windsor with the shuttle service to Slough during June 1969.

Above and below: Two pictures of DMUs at Bath taken in May 1969. The first shows a Class 119 on a Weymouth to Bristol service shortly after leaving Bath Station and crossing the viaduct through the city. The second shows a Class 120 standing in Bath Spa Station with a Weymouth to Bristol service.

This scene at Shrewsbury Station, taken in September 1969, shows a Class 120 unit waiting to depart with a Central Wales line service to Swansea. The DMUs working this line were among the few BR trains to be fitted with headlights at this time, which assisted drivers through the bleak country through which this service passed.

The driver of a Park Royal Class 103 DMU gives up the single line token as his train arrives at Aberystwyth from Shrewsbury on 1 September 1970. Just visible to the right is the old GWR engine shed, which was still in use by BR's only steam engines, which worked the narrow gauge line to Devils Bridge.

The morning mist is clearing on 3 September 1970 as Metro-Cammell Class 101 DMU arrives at Porthmadog with a Pwllheli to Machynlleth service. The station area still has a full complement of semaphore signals, and the goods yard looks to be busy, with coal wagons waiting to be unloaded, a ferry van, and a line of gunpowder vans – their contents destined for the local quarries.

Taken from a train crossing the Great Western main line at North Acton, a Class 116 forms a local train for Paddington as a Class 31-hauled freight from Acton Yard climbs up to join the North London line and follow our train.

A lengthy commuter train, formed of two Class 123s and a Class 116 unit, passes Royal Oak Station shortly after departure from Paddington in March 1972.

A pair of 120 units speed towards Newport through the site of St Devereux Station with a train bound for Newport and Cardiff on 6 April 1974.

Above and below: Two scenes at Liskeard showing first of all a Class 120 crossing the 150-foot-high Liskeard Viaduct with a Plymouth to Penzance train on 17 October 1975. The second shows a Penzance to Plymouth train formed of a Class 119 arriving at Liskeard Station on 18 October 1975.

Above: Parcels are loaded into the goods section of a Class 119 unit at Newquay Station before departure for Par on 17 October 1975. The branch to Newquay is one of four in Cornwall to survive the Beeching cuts.

Right: The branch line train from Liskeard to Looe, formed of a Class 119 set, pauses at Coombe halt during its thirty-minute journey on 18 October 1975. The line was to close under the Beeching plan, but was reprieved two weeks before closure and survives to this day. Just visible in the background is the 147-foot-high Moorswater Viaduct, which carries the Cornish main line.

A Class 108 with an additional Metro-Cammell car inserted in the middle leaves Ruabon on a Chester to Shrewsbury service on 5 June 1976.

A Class 116 stands at Oxford Station with a stopping service to Reading on 29 May 1977. Oxford is an important stop on the ex-GWR main lines from Paddington to Birmingham and Hereford. There has been a station here since 1844 and the current one dates from 1990.

The tide is in at Dawlish as a Class 120 departs on a Plymouth to Exeter service on 15 July 1977.

A Metro-Cammell Class 101 unit departs from Shrewsbury for Wolverhampton in July 1977 and is passing a very unusual signal. In the right-hand background the large signal box can be seen, which is still in use today.

A Class 116 unit in the short-lived white livery leaves Iver with a Slough to Paddington local service on 1 March 1979.

Above and below: Two pictures taken at Weston Rhyn, which is on the Chester to Shrewsbury line just to the south of the Welsh border. The first picture shows a 116/101 hybrid DMU passing the site of the station, which closed in 1960, with the signal box and level crossing in the picture. The top half, the levers and other working parts from the box were acquired by the Llangollen Railway after the box closed in August 1991, and has been rebuilt at Carrog. The second picture shows 150 119 passing the loops to the north of the station site. Both pictures were taken on 12 October 1990 and show Shrewsbury to Wolverhampton services.

A busy scene at Reading showing 165 108 leaving for Paddington on 17 April 2002. Also in the picture, another 165 on the up through road, a 125 in platform 2, and a Southern train to Waterloo formed of 3409. The new footbridge is visible, which opened in 1989, along with major improvements to the station entrance area. More drastic changes were to take place from 2009 to 2015, which involved alterations to the platforms, the track layout, and erection of the overhead masts and wiring for the Western electrification.

Two Class 166 Network Turbo Express units, introduced in 1992 by British Rail for use on Great Western longer distance services in the Thames Valley, are seen at Paddington on 17 April 2002.

Above and below: Another former Great Western line was the Paddington to Birmingham route, which passed through Princes Risborough where Class 168 215 is seen departing for London Marylebone, past the former GWR signal box, with a Chiltern Railways train from Birmingham Moor Street on 5 June 2003. Also seen at Princes Risborough on the same day is vintage Class 121 020 single-car diesel unit, nicknamed Bubblecars, forming the branch line service to and from Aylesbury.

Above right and right: Two Cross Country Class 221 Bombardier Super Voyager trains, which were introduced in 2001, are seen at Oxford. They are working services to and from Bournemouth to the north of England. A little later Thames Trains Class 165 120 is ready to depart for Paddington with a semi-fast service on 5 June 2003.

The view from the Warren Road bridge overlooking the GW main line as it passes through the famous Sonning Cutting, which reaches a depth of around 60 feet. The next bridge is London Road bridge and beyond that the cutting finishes at the approach to Reading Station. A Class 166 heads for Paddington and another disappears towards Reading on 3 June 2004.

Brunel's Paddington Station, which dates from 1854, is seen in this picture taken on 3 June 2004 before the start of the major refurbishment, which started in 2010 and took six years to complete. From left to right are two Heathrow Express Class 332 units, which date from 1997, and then three First Great Western Class 180 Adelante sets, 107, 114 and 106, which were introduced from 2000 and were mainly used on services to Oxford, Worcester and Hereford. Unfortunately they suffered from engine problems, and were transferred to other operators in 2009.

Above and below: Two pictures taken on the Cambrian Coast line on 18 September 2006. First is 158 824 passing the Talyllyn Railway Station as it leaves Tywyn for Machynlleth, and the second shows another service crossing the famous Barmouth Viaduct. The Grade II listed structure gained notoriety in 1980 when it was discovered to be infested with marine woodworm and was thought to be beyond repair. As this would have meant the closure of the line, it was decided to make expensive repairs, which closed the bridge for six months but assured the line's future.

On 16 September 2006 Class 158 834 waits in Aberystwyth Station to depart on the afternoon Cambrian Lines service. The two-car train will join up at Machynlleth with the section from Pwllheli and continue to Wolverhampton.

Weston-super-Mare is a seaside town on the Bristol Channel that was a very popular resort serving the Bristol area. The busy station covered a large site with many platforms and sidings, which have long disappeared. Standing under its unusual footbridge, 221 123 calls with a Cross Country service for Paignton on 29 February 2008.

Above and below: Two pictures taken at Bristol Temple Meads on 1 March 2008. First 143 611 stands under the magnificent roof of the station with the 10.49 to Avonmouth, and the second shows 150 121 arriving at the west end with a local service from Weston-super-Mare. The original station was built in 1840, but was gradually enlarged to cope as traffic increased, reaching its present size in 1935.

175 004 is about to depart from Newport (Mon.) with an afternoon service to Holyhead on 23 July 2018.

166 219, in the latest GWR green livery, departs from Newport with a train for Cardiff on 23 July 2018.

153 320 waits at Cardiff to take up its next working on 23 July 2018.

142 002 departs from Cardiff with a Penarth to Bargoed service during the afternoon of 23 July 2018.

800 011, nearest the camera, has just arrived at Cardiff with a train from Paddington as, in the background, 800 016 waits to depart with a Paddington service on 23 July 2018.

West Midlands Railway 172 182 departs from Smethwick Galton Bridge with a Worcester service on 9 June 2019.